YESTERDAY'S HEROES

By John N. Smallwood, Jr.

SCHOLASTIC INC.

New York   Toronto   London   Auckland   Sydney
Mexico City   New Delhi   Hong Kong

Dedicated to Teale, Ian and Brayden—
you are the future. Love, Uncle Johnny

PHOTO CREDITS
NBA Entertainment Photos
Front Cover (Erving), 21, 40, 41: Ken Regan. Front Cover (Kidd): Barry Gossage.
Front Cover (Garnett), 60 (bottom right): Rocky Widner. Back Cover (Abdul-
Jabbar), 17, 49, 50, 52, 60 (top right, top left), 65, 66, 69: Andrew D. Bernstein.
Back Cover (shoe/ball): Steven Freeman. 4: Fernando Medina. 13: Dick Raphael.
25: George Kalinsky. 28, 35, 36, 45, 55: NBA Photo Library. 42: Ron Koch.
57: Jerry Wachter. 58: Ray Amati. 60 (bottom left): Steve Woltman.
71: David Sherman. 73: Lou Capozzola. 74: Sam Forencich.

6, 8, 11, 14, 33: Hall of Fame.
Front Cover (Lloyd, Cooper, Robertson), 19, 39: AP/Wide World.

PHOTO CREDITS: INSERT SECTION
NBA Entertainment Photos
I: Dick Raphael. II, IV: Neil Leifer. III: Robert Lewis. V: Dale Tait.
VI: Andrew D. Bernstein. VII: Andy Hayt. VIII: Nathaniel S. Butler.

ISBN 0-439-24110-3

© 2001 by NBA Properties, Inc.
All rights reserved. Published by Scholastic Inc.

12 11 10 9 8 7 6 5 4 3 2 1   1 2 3 4 5 6/0 1

Printed in the U.S.A.
First Scholastic printing, February 2001
Book Design: Michael Malone

TABLE OF CONTENTS

Stephon Marbury

INTRODUCTION

The crowd at the Air Canada Centre rises to its feet, looking for another spectacular dunk by the "Half-Man, Half-Amazing" Vince Carter of the Toronto Raptors. In Los Angeles, superstars Shaquille O'Neal and Kobe Bryant are the new dynamic duo of the Showtime Lakers. And in Philadelphia, "The Answer" is always the 76ers' super guard Allen Iverson.

Of all the pro sports leagues in the United States, the National Basketball Association has the most African-American players. From today's stars—Kobe Bryant, Vince Carter, Allen Iverson, Stephon Marbury of the New Jersey Nets and Ray Allen of the Milwaukee Bucks—to legendary players like Wilt Chamberlain, Julius "Dr. J" Erving, Earvin "Magic" Johnson and, of course, Michael Jordan, African-American players have always been some of the NBA's best players and the fans' favorites.

Today, it is not unusual to see 10 African-American players on a court at the same time during a game, but there was a time when there were no African-American players in the NBA.

The NBA traces its roots to the Basketball Association of America, which began in 1946. At that time, separation of the races was still the norm for most of America. So even though African-Americans were playing basketball with white players in many colleges, they were not allowed to play in the NBA because of the color of their skin.

5

The Rens

There were professional basketball leagues besides the BAA, but they were also segregated. Unlike baseball, in which the Negro League gave African-American players a place to play, there was no formal league for black basketball players. To make a living playing their sport, the best African-American players often formed teams and would travel from city to city to play exhibition games, often against white teams. This was called barnstorming.

The greatest barnstorming team of all time was the New York Renaissance Five. The Rens, as they were called, was an all African-American team formed in 1922 by Robert Douglas in Harlem, New

York. In the 1930s, the team featured center Charles "Tarzan" Cooper, Eyre "Bruiser" Satch and Wee Willie Smith, and was considered the best professional team in the world.

But because they were African-American, the Rens' players often had to suffer through many bad things just to play their games. Sometimes, white fans would spit on them and call them names. They often had to drive hundreds of miles to and from games so they could find a safe place to sleep. Still, the Rens played on. They once won 88 games in a row. "We would not let anyone deny us our right to make a living," Eric Illidge, a member of the Rens, once said.

Another famous African-American barnstorming team, which is still around today, was the Harlem Globetrotters. Before they became known as the "Clown Princes of Basketball," the Globetrotters, who were actually from Chicago, were one of the best barnstorming teams around. There were only limited opportunities for African-American basketball players, and none offered the fame, publicity and opportunities that the NBA did.

But when African-American baseball great Jackie Robinson signed a contract with the Brooklyn Dodgers on August 29, 1945, American sports fans knew it was just a matter of time before many African-American players would be in the Major Leagues.

Reece "Goose" Tatum

Back then, however, basketball was not as popular as baseball, and the people who were starting the NBA—which was actually called the Basketball Association of America at first—were afraid that white fans would not buy tickets to see African-American basketball players. So instead of taking a chance that their customers might get angry and not buy tickets, the owners decided they would not allow African-American players in the league in order to avoid problems.

Even after Jackie Robinson played for the Dodgers on Opening Day, April 15, 1947, and UCLA basketball star Don Barksdale made history by becoming the first African-American to play in the Olympics in 1948, the NBA still had no African-Americans during its first four seasons.

But by the end of the 1949–50 season, everyone in the NBA knew that things were about to change.

CHAPTER 1

The Trailblazers

Earl Lloyd was more than 70 years old when the new millennium began, but he remembers the night of October 31, 1950, like it was yesterday. How could he forget the Halloween night when he made NBA history?

"I think the people in the crowd must have thought I was wearing a Halloween costume," Lloyd laughed, remembering the night he became the first African-American to play in an NBA game. "They had never seen any player like me before." In the winter of 1950, Earl Lloyd, Chuck Cooper and Nat "Sweetwater" Clifton were the three men who finally brought color to the NBA.

Chuck Cooper walked through the door first when he was drafted by the Boston Celtics first-year coach Arnold "Red" Auerbach. "When I looked at a player, I didn't look to see what color they were," Auerbach said in the book *The NBA at 50*. "What did I care? I was trying to build a team and Chuck Cooper was a good prospect."

Cooper had grown up in Pittsburgh, Pennsylvania, and was an all-city player in high school who stayed near home to attend college at Duquesne University before being drafted into the NBA.

In 1950, Nat Clifton was a member of the Harlem Globetrotters. A 6-7 forward from Chicago who got the nickname "Sweetwater" because he loved soda pop as a

Earl Lloyd

child, Clifton had joined the Globetrotters after serving in the Army. But when the New York Knicks offered him a job, he quit the Globetrotters and became the first African-American to sign an NBA contract.

But the honor of being the first to play in an NBA game as an African-American belongs to Earl Lloyd. Lloyd, who was nicknamed the "Big Cat," was a 6-6 forward who had starred at West Virginia State University before he became the ninth-round draft pick of the Washington Capitols.

Because the NBA schedule had the Capitols starting the 1950 season a day before the Celtics and Knicks, Lloyd made history when he entered the game against the Rochester Royals in Rochester, New York, on Halloween night. Cooper played for the Celtics the next day.

Although they were the first African-Americans in the NBA, Clifton, Cooper and Lloyd were not as famous as baseball's Robinson. They did not face the same amount of anger as Robinson did when he broke Major League baseball's color barrier.

"I don't think my situation was anything like Jackie Robinson's situation," Earl Lloyd said. "Jackie Robinson played in a very hostile environment, where even some of his teammates didn't want him to be around. In basketball, folks were already used to seeing integrated teams in college. They looked at it differently."

But that did not mean that Lloyd, Clifton and Cooper did not have rough experiences. Once, after a game in Fort Wayne, Indiana, Lloyd and a white teammate, John "Red" Kerr, were walking off the court together after a victory. "I had my arm around Earl, and some fans just

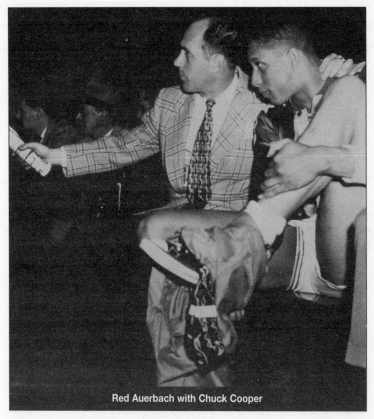

Red Auerbach with Chuck Cooper

spit on us," said Kerr. "It wasn't because we had won the game. They were spitting on Earl."

Sometimes, Cooper, Lloyd and Clifton were not allowed to stay in the same hotels or eat at the same restaurants as their white teammates. "I remember in Fort Wayne, we stayed at a hotel where they let me sleep, but they wouldn't let me eat," Lloyd said. "They didn't want anyone to see me. I figured if they let me sleep there, I was at least halfway home. You have to remem-

Nat "Sweetwater" Clifton with Joe Lapchick (Knicks head coach)

ber that I grew up in segregated Virginia, so I had seen that stuff before. It didn't make me bitter. If you let yourself become bitter, it will eat away at you inside. If adversity doesn't kill you, it makes you a better person."

It was the coaches and teammates of Lloyd, Clifton and Cooper who made the three African-American players feel like they were not alone in their struggles. Once, when the Boston Celtics were playing an exhibition game in Charlotte, North Carolina, Cooper was not allowed to stay at the same hotel as the rest of the team. After the game, future Hall of Fame point guard Bob Cousy, who was also a rookie in 1950 and Cooper's roommate, decided he would take the train out of Charlotte with Cooper and stay wherever he stayed.

"It was a traumatic experience for Chuck because it was the first time he had to face blatant racism," Cousy told NBA.com. "I told Coach Auerbach Chuck and I were leaving. Throughout the season, Chuck faced isolated instances of racism at other hotels and restaurants.

"Everyone on the Celtics liked Chuck because he was a highly intelligent, sensitive young man who was an intense competitor. The fact that he was black was a non-issue in my mind and in the minds of our teammates, although it was to others." Cousy said he wasn't necessarily trying to make a statement about supporting his friend because he was African-American. "To me, it was always just two teammates hanging out together."

In their first year, Cooper had the best season of the three African-American trailblazers. He played in 65 games, scored 615 points, had 491 rebounds and 174 assists. He played four seasons with the Celtics before moving to the Milwaukee Hawks. The Hawks moved to St. Louis the next season and Cooper, who was the only African-American on the team, was traded to the Fort Wayne Pistons.

In his six-year NBA career, Cooper averaged 6.7 points. "I do feel a sense of accomplishment in a very modest way," Cooper once said of being one of the first African-Americans in the NBA. "I can't help but feel proud. But when I was playing, I never thought about that. I was more concerned with just making the team."

Clifton spent seven seasons in New York, and became one of the Knicks' most popular players. He averaged 10 points and 8.2 rebounds for his career.

Although Lloyd was the first to play, he only played in six more games as a rookie. He was drafted into military service that same year and then, two months after he became the first African-American player in the NBA, the Washington Capitols folded on January 9, 1951. But four years later, Lloyd, along with Jim Tucker, became the first African-American players to join an NBA championship team the year the 1954–55 Syracuse Nationals won the title.

"When you're seventy years old, if you start telling people that you were the first black man to play in the NBA, people look at you like you're crazy," said Lloyd, who retired from playing in 1960. During the 1971–72 season, he became the first African-American head coach of the Detroit Pistons.

Chuck Cooper, Nat "Sweetwater" Clifton and Earl Lloyd don't hold any NBA records. But it is because of them that almost every NBA record is now held by an African-American player.

"We owe everything to men like them," Philadelphia 76ers guard Eric Snow said about the first African-American players. "It's hard just to become a professional athlete. I can't even imagine what it was like for them to have to play when they couldn't stay with their teams or eat in the same places as their teammates.

"Those are things we never had to go through, just not being accepted by people because of the color of your skin. Sometimes we take for granted that we can go here

Eric Snow

or eat there. We can do that now, but back then we couldn't. Back then you were looked at as an entirely different person when you took your uniform off."

Then Came the Giants

In 1950 the NBA allowed African-American players into the league, but there was still an unwritten rule limiting the number of African-Americans on a team, and none played where they could be stars.

The league's superstars were white players like Minneapolis Lakers center George Mikan, Boston Celtics guards Bill Sharman and Bob Cousy, Philadelphia Warriors forward Paul Arizin and Syracuse Nationals center Dolph Schayes. Don Barksdale, the 1948 Olympian who came into the league with the Baltimore Bullets in 1951, became the first African-American player to make an NBA All-Star team in 1953. But most of the early African-American players were role players rather than stars.

"If you look at the early days, there were not a lot of blacks," Hall of Fame guard Oscar Robertson once said. "A lot of blacks who were great players did not make teams because (the league) did not want too many."

NBA coaches had a traditional approach to how the game should be played, but because African-American players had not been allowed in organized professional leagues before, they introduced the NBA to a very different style. The "black" style of basketball was fast and

Oscar Robertson

quick. The players jumped higher and made flashier passes. Even though it was more fun to watch, this style scared a lot of coaches who wanted the game played at a slower pace. But the league soon discovered that fans were bored with the slow pace of NBA games.

In an effort to make the game quicker and more interesting, the NBA created the 24-second shot clock for the 1954–55 season. Two seasons later, the first great African-American superstar came into the league.

Bill Russell was a 6-9 center who had led the University of San Francisco to back-to-back NCAA titles in 1955 and 1956. He had also helped the United States win the 1956 Olympic gold medal. He got so good at rebounding in college that the NCAA changed its rules so other teams would have a better chance against San Francisco.

Bill Russell was selected third overall by the St. Louis Hawks in the 1956 NBA Draft, but was immediately traded to the Boston Celtics for two players—Ed MacCauley and Cliff Hagan.

Russell brought a new weapon to NBA defense—the blocked shot. He was the first player who helped his team generate offense out of great defensive play. His ability to block shots and rebound triggered the Celtics' famous fast break.

"Nobody had ever blocked shots in the pros before Bill Russell came along," said Boston Celtics legendary coach Red Auerbach. "He upset everybody."

In Russell's rookie season, the Celtics won the first of their record 16 NBA titles. On November 16, 1957, he grabbed 32 rebounds in one half against Philadelphia, a record that still stands today. By his third season, Russell was the best player in the NBA. In 1958, he became the first African-American to be named the league's Most Valuable Player.

Wilt Chamberlain

Russell was a giant, but the NBA was about to meet someone even bigger: Wilton Norman Chamberlain, who stood 7-1 and weighed 275 pounds. No one could ever dominate a basketball game the way Wilt could. Chamberlain left the University of Kansas after his junior year and played the 1958 season with the Harlem Globetrotters because NBA rules prevented him from joining the league until his college class graduated. He joined the Philadelphia Warriors in 1959, and was immediately better than everybody else. Basketball had never seen a player like "Wilt the Stilt."

"There will be a period of orientation for me like there is for every newcomer in the NBA," Wilt said when he signed his contract in October 1959. "But I think in the long run, I'll be able to handle myself man-to-man with anyone in the league." Wilt was right. He led the league in scoring (37.6 points) and rebounding (27.0) his first season and was named both Rookie of the Year and league MVP.

Through his first seven seasons, Wilt never averaged less than 33 points and 22 rebounds. During the 1961–62 season he averaged 50.4 points and 25.7 rebounds.

He still holds more than 50 NBA records.

"Wilt was the most unbelievable center to ever play the game in terms of domination and intimidation," said former Los Angeles Lakers general manager and Hall of Fame player Jerry West. "There have been a lot of players that have played as well at different positions, but there's no one that's ever played the game better than Wilt Chamberlain."

Because Bill Russell and Wilt Chamberlain were so much better than everyone else, some other important African-American players who entered the league around the same time often get overlooked. Guard Sam Jones joined the Boston Celtics in 1957, and guard K.C. Jones followed him a season later. In 1958, guard Hal Greer joined the Syracuse Nationals and Guy Rodgers joined the Philadelphia Warriors.

These players are important because they were guards. Before they entered the league, a lot of white coaches and fans believed that African-Americans could not be guards because they were not smart enough to run a team. Sam Jones, K.C. Jones, Hal Greer and Guy Rodgers proved that was not true, and their success opened the door into the NBA for African-Americans who were not tall and strong. They helped show NBA fans that "black style" wasn't just fun basketball, but that it was also smart basketball.

"A lot of young people don't really know how good those players were," Philadelphia 76ers superstar guard Allen Iverson has said about his predecessors. "A lot of the things we do now is because they were able to do it first." The door to the NBA had finally opened for African-Americans, and further success was just around the corner.

KEY MOMENTS OF THE 1950s

1950—Chuck Cooper is drafted in the second round by the Boston Celtics. He is the first African-American player to drafted by an NBA team. In the ninth round, the Washington Capitols draft Earl Lloyd.

1950—Nat "Sweetwater" Clifton of the Harlem Globetrotters signs with the New York Knicks, becoming the first African-American to sign with an NBA team.

October 31, 1950—In Rochester, New York, Earl Lloyd plays in a game against the Rochester Royals, becoming the first African-American to play in an NBA game.

January 13, 1953—Boston Celtics forward Don Barksdale who, in 1948, was the first African-American to play on a U.S. Olympic team, becomes the first African-American player to make a NBA All-Star team.

April 10, 1955—With African-American players Earl Lloyd and Jim Tucker on the roster, the Syracuse Nationals defeat the Fort Wayne Pistons 92–91 in Game 7 to win the NBA championship.

1956—University of San Francisco center Bill Russell is selected third overall in the NBA Draft by the St. Louis Hawks, then traded to the Boston Celtics.

1956–57—Rochester Royals forward Maurice Stokes averages 17.4 rebounds to become the first African-American to win an NBA statistical title.

1958—With the first pick in the 1958 NBA Draft, the Minneapolis Lakers make Seattle University forward Elgin Baylor the first African-American to be picked number one overall in the NBA Draft.

1958—Averaging 16.6 points and 22.2 rebounds, Boston Celtics center Bill Russell becomes the first African-American to be named NBA Most Valuable Player.

April 12, 1958—The St. Louis Hawks defeat the Boston Celtics, 110–109, in Game 7 of the NBA Finals. They were the last all-white team to win an NBA championship.

1959—The St. Louis Hawks acquire Sihugo Green from the Cincinnati Royals, becoming the last NBA team to acquire an African-American player.

1959—Kansas University center Wilt Chamberlain, who left school a year early to join the Harlem Globetrotters, is drafted as a territorial pick by the Philadelphia Warriors.

Civil Rights and the 1960s

By the start of the 1960s, the two best players in the NBA—Wilt Chamberlain and Bill Russell—were African-Americans. The game had drastically changed and would never return to the way it once was. After Russell won his first MVP in 1958, only four white players have been named MVP since—Bob Pettit of the St. Louis Hawks in 1959, Dave Cowens of the Boston Celtics in 1973, Bill Walton of the Portland Trail Blazers in 1978 and Larry Bird of the Boston Celtics in 1984, 1985 and 1986.

In 1958, the St. Louis Hawks became the last all-white team to win an NBA championship. During his rookie season, Chamberlain became the first African-American to win the NBA scoring title. In the 40 seasons since then only three white players have won scoring titles—Rick Barry of the San Francisco Warriors in 1966–67; Jerry West of the Los Angeles Lakers in 1969–70 and Pete Maravich of the New Orleans Jazz in 1976–77.

The great games between the giants—Russell and Chamberlain—helped the NBA grow in popularity during the 1960s. While Chamberlain won most of the individual battles, Russell came away with almost all of the big victories.

24

Elgin Baylor

When Russell retired in 1969, he had been a member of 11 NBA championship teams. No other athlete in American professional sports has won as many championships.

Chamberlain won only one championship while Russell was playing, but Chamberlain's 1966–67 Philadelphia 76ers are considered by many to be the greatest team in NBA history.

"Winning is the only thing I really cared about," Russell said. "When I left my childhood, I learned that individual awards were mostly political. There are no politics in that, only numbers. It's the most democratic thing in the world. You either win or lose."

The 1960s had a lot of great African-American players. Before Phoenix Suns guard Jason Kidd and Orlando Magic forward Grant Hill were getting triple-doubles, Cincinnati Royals guard Oscar Robertson invented the statistic. During the 1961–62 season, Oscar averaged a triple-double for the entire year.

"Right now in baseball, people talk a lot about if Mark McGwire will break Hank Aaron's home run record," Kidd said. "That may be possible, but I think what Oscar Robertson did by averaging a triple-double for a whole season is something that we will never see again. That will stand forever. I've always dreamed of trying to do it, but you'd have to have the ball bounce right for you the entire season. That's just not going to happen."

Before Toronto Raptor Vince Carter started skywalking, Los Angeles Lakers star Elgin Baylor first proved basketball players could fly. Elgin averaged 27.4 points and 13.5 rebounds in his 14-year career.

In 1960, the Minneapolis Lakers moved to Los

Angeles, bringing Baylor, their great African-American star, with them. In 1962, the Philadelphia Warriors and the great Chamberlain moved to San Francisco. The NBA had moved to the West Coast, and two of the league's best African-American players showed a whole new audience how good professional basketball could be.

But while the 1960s were a time of great advancement on the court for African-American players, it was a time of turmoil off the court. Because of the Civil Rights movement, American society was going through great changes. African-Americans were demanding to be treated equally and with the same respect as white Americans.

Many of the African-American players in the NBA were very interested in participating in the social movements going on around them and, instead of quietly accepting the injustices going on around them, they spoke out against them.

"We played an exhibition game in Lubbock, Texas, and we stayed at a Holiday Inn," Robertson recalled, remembering his experience in the hotel restaurant. "We got there and they put us in a little section and pulled a huge curtain across the room. "Maybe I was overly sensitive, maybe I wasn't. But I said 'If you don't move the curtain, I'm not going to play.' There was no reason for that curtain. There was hardly anyone in the restaurant. They did it because there were black players on our team. If you talk to other guys, they were going through the same thing in the sixties."

Oscar Robertson had been scarred by racism. As a high school player in Indianapolis, Indiana, he led Crispus Attucks High to the state championship, but the parade

Lenny Wilkens

for the team was held outside of town. He was the first African-American player at the University of Cincinnati, and the school often made him stay alone at college dormitories if a hotel would not let him stay. But Robertson's refusal to accept injustice made him the perfect man to become president of the NBA Players' Association in 1966.

Robertson wasn't alone in his fight. Bill Russell was a star for the Celtics, but he played in one of the most segregated cities in the nation. Because Bill refused to allow himself to be treated with any less respect than any other person, and because he was not afraid to speak out against injustices, many whites considered him threatening or ungrateful.

The sports media, which had no African-American reporters at that time, was particularly critical of African-American athletes. In 1961, Russell was harshly criticized by the media when he boycotted a Boston Celtics exhibition game in Lexington, Kentucky, because he and two of his teammates were refused service in a hotel coffee shop. In an interview with *Sports Illustrated* in 1963, Russell said, "I don't consider anything I've done as a contribution to society. I consider playing professional basketball the most shallow thing in the world.

"Some black entertainers try to show whites that they are nice people. All of us are nice people but this isn't a popularity contest. I don't care if a waitress likes me when I go into a restaurant. All I want is something to eat."

Baylor, who is now the general manager of the Los Angeles Clippers, also boycotted a game in Charleston, West Virginia, when a hotel clerk looked at him and two other African-Americans on the team and said, "We can't take those three. We run a respectable hotel." When a white teammate—Rod "Hot Rod" Hundley—tried to convince Baylor to play anyway, Baylor responded, "Rod, I'm a human being. I am not an animal put in a cage and let out for show."

Detroit Pistons All-Star guard Jerry Stackhouse said that these stories "really opened my eyes to how difficult it was to be an African-American athlete at that time. We've come so far so fast that it's sometimes easy to forget how things were. The league has grown, and players today receive great benefits, but that's because of the sacrifices and struggles that so many great players went through."

As the Civil Rights movement grew in society, so too were African-American basketball players becoming more assertive Civil Rights supporters. In 1968, several top collegiate African-American players like Lew Alcindor (now Kareem Abdul-Jabbar) and Mike Warren of UCLA, Wes Unseld of Louisville, Elvin Hayes of Houston and Bob Lanier of St. Bonaventure declined to represent the United States at the 1968 Olympics in Mexico City. Olympic team coach Hank Iba called them "bad citizens."

As African-American players began to outnumber white players in the league, the NBA had little choice but to pay attention to the issues of African-Americans. On April 5, 1968, the day after the great Civil Rights leader, the reverend Dr. Martin Luther King, Jr., was assassinated in Memphis, Tennessee, the Celtics and Philadelphia 76ers were scheduled to play the first game of the Eastern Conference Finals. The NBA decided to play the game, but not before it asked the opinion of both Russell and Chamberlain.

When Red Auerbach retired as head coach of the Boston Celtics in 1966, he immediately named Russell as his replacement. Russell became the first African-American to become a head coach in either the NBA, National Football League, National Hockey League or Major League Baseball. He won two NBA championships as the player-coach of the Celtics before retiring in 1969.

Before the start of the 1969–70 season, Lenny Wilkens was named player-head coach of the Seattle SuperSonics and, later that season, Al Attles was named player-head coach of the San Francisco Warriors.

"I was really a novelty when I became a player-coach because only Bill Russell had done it previously," said Wilkens who, along with legendary UCLA coach John Wooden, is one of two people to be in the Basketball Hall of Fame as both a player and coach. "The biggest problem I felt was that guys I had played with all of a sudden wanted to take advantage of me. I had to really make an effort to get on them to be in shape and work hard."

The NBA had three African-American head coaches, and both Russell and Attles won NBA championships before any of the other professional sports leagues allowed an African-American to become a head coach. By the end of the 1960s, the influence of African-Americans in the NBA was established and growing.

"When you think of the best players of all time, you of course have Michael Jordan," said Los Angeles Lakers star Kobe Bryant. "But I'd say you also have to remember players like Wilt Chamberlain, Oscar Robertson and Bill Russell. There are so many great players that people have forgotten."

KEY MOMENTS OF THE 1960s

1960—After averaging 37.6 points and 27.0 rebounds, the Philadelphia Warriors' Wilt Chamberlain is named Rookie of the Year and Most Valuable Player. He is also the first African-American to lead the league in scoring.

1960–61—Cincinnati Royals rookie guard Oscar "The Big O" Robertson averages 9.7 assists to lead the league, proving that African-Americans could be great point guards, as well as forwards.

October 1961—Boston Celtics center Bill Russell refuses to play in an exhibition game in Lexington, Kentucky, after he and two teammates are refused service in a restaurant because they are African-American.

1961–62—Cincinnati Royal guard Oscar Robertson averages a triple-double for the season (30.8 points, 12.5 rebounds and 11.4 assists)

March 2, 1962—Wilt Chamberlain of the Philadelphia Warriors sets an NBA record by scoring 100 points in a game against the New York Knicks.

April 1966—Arnold "Red" Auerbach retires as head coach of the Boston Celtics. As executive vice president of the team, Auerbach names Bill Russell as his successor, making Russell the first African-American head coach in the NBA.

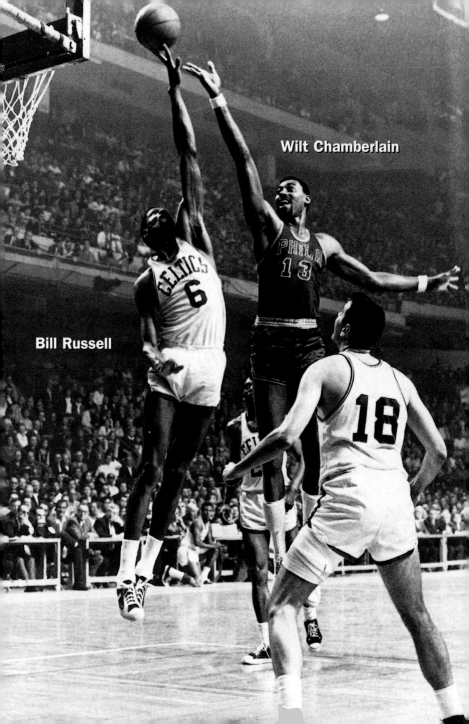

Wilt Chamberlain

Bill Russell

Elgin Baylor

Oscar Robertson

Julius Erving

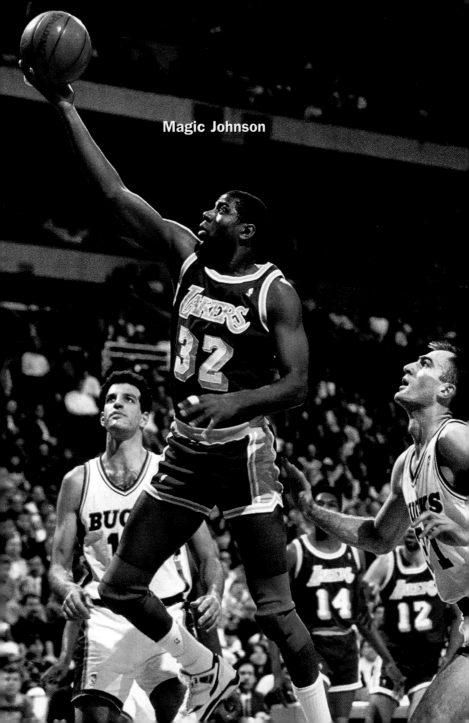

Magic Johnson

Michael Jordan

Shaquille O'Neal

Vince Carter

VINCE CARTER

CHAPTER 4

The Forgotten Boy Wonder

Today in the NBA, many star players leave college early to become professional players and some, like Kevin

Spencer Haywood

Garnett, Kobe Bryant and Tracy McGrady, came into the league directly from high school. But there was a time when players were not allowed in the league until their collegiate class had graduated. That's why Wilt Chamberlain played one season with the Harlem Globetrotters before entering the NBA.

But in 1971, one African-American player fought that rule and changed the face of the NBA forever. Spencer Haywood was born in Silver City, Mississippi, the son of a poor mother who worked in the cotton fields.

"Even though slavery had been outlawed for almost one hundred years, it still existed in certain parts of the country," Haywood said about his youth in a documentary on the HBO television program *Real Sports*. "My mother knew that I didn't have a good future ahead of me in Mississippi so she said, 'I have to let you go now.' I left home when I was fifteen."

Haywood was sent to live with relatives in Detroit, Michigan, and he soon grew into a 6-9 basketball star. He played at Pershing High School, then went to Trinidad State Junior College in Colorado before becoming one of the most sought-after recruits in the country.

Unlike several other prominent African-American players, he did not boycott the 1968 Olympics, and helped the United States win the gold medal. "I was like, wow," Spencer said of the 1968 Olympics. "Three years ago I was a slave and now I'm a hero for the United States Olympic team."

Spencer accepted a scholarship to play at Detroit University after the school promised that it would hire his high school coach and legal guardian Will Robinson as the first African-American coach in NCAA Division I history. But after Spencer played the 1968–69 season for Detroit, averaging 32.1 points and 21.5 rebounds, the school broke its promise and did not hire Robinson.

In protest, Haywood left Detroit and, at age 20, signed a professional contract with the Denver Rockets of the American Basketball Association. The ABA, which was the other major basketball league in the United States, was struggling for star players and decided to drop its rule against signing college underclassmen.

Spencer played one season for the Rockets and was named MVP and Rookie of the Year of the ABA. But he

Spencer Haywood

Spencer Haywood

then canceled his contract with Denver. Although the NBA still had its rule against allowing players to play before their collegiate class had graduated, Seattle SuperSonics owner Sam Schulman asked for permission to sign Spencer.

When the other team owners voted 15–2 not to allow Seattle to sign Spencer to a contract, the SuperSonics did it anyway. "I thought it was a stupid rule to make a young man who had talent to wait for years to make a living," Schulman said. The SuperSonics gave Spencer a $1.5 million contract for six years, but the NBA went to court to prevent him from playing.

The league got court rulings to prevent Spencer from playing in games while the issue was being fought out in court. On March 30, 1971, a Federal judge in Los Angeles ruled that the NBA's four-year college stay rule was illegal because it violated the Sherman Anti-Trust Act.

Spencer's historic fight made it possible for talented players to enter the NBA whenever they wanted, which is something that many of today's players take advantage of.

CHAPTER 5

The 1970s – Kareem, Clyde, Doc and Trouble

When the 1970s began, most of the top players in the NBA were African-American. It had taken just 20 years for the league to go from one that did not allow African-Americans to play to one that was dominated by African-American players.

Bill Russell had retired in 1969, and Wilt Chamberlain was finishing up his Hall of Fame career with the Los Angeles Lakers. But in 1969, another African-American giant had entered the NBA.

He came into the league in 1969 as Lew Alcindor, but in 1971, after becoming a Muslim, he changed his name to Kareem Abdul-Jabbar. Kareem was set to live up to the standards set by Russell and Chamberlain. He had led UCLA to an 88–2 record and an NCAA title in each of the three seasons he played varsity basketball.

The Milwaukee Bucks made him the first overall pick in the 1969 NBA Draft. Kareem used the most famous shot in basketball—The Sky Hook—to become the league's all-time leading scorer. "[The Sky Hook is] the

Kareem Abdul-Jabbar and Oscar Robertson

Earl Monroe

greatest weapon of one person who's ever been an athlete in any sport," said Miami Heat coach Pat Riley, who coached Kareem with the Lakers.

In 1971, Kareem teamed with the legendary Oscar Robertson to win the NBA title for the Milwaukee Bucks. Kareem was traded to the Los Angeles Lakers in 1975, and although he remained one of the best players in the league, he would not be a champion again until 1980.

"The remarkable thing about [Kareem] is, here's a man who played twenty years," Los Angeles Lakers Hall of Fame player and former general manager Jerry West said, reflecting on Abdul-Jabbar's career. "He came into the league when basketball was just growing. He left the game when it was at the height of its popularity. During that time, he played against some people who were in the Hall of Fame, and he played against today's young lions. I don't think he saw anyone who scared him. He taught a lot of lessons to a lot of young centers in this league."

The 1970s was called the "Me Decade," and Americans were all about being flashy and having personality. That was the perfect setting for one of the flashiest athletes the world has ever seen. Walt "Clyde" Frazier was born to play in New York City. He was the definition of cool. From his tailored suits, full-length fur coats, stylish wide-brim hats and fancy cars, "Clyde" had the perfect style for the Big Apple. And to top it all off, he could play, too.

"I think it was an era where people were looking for individuality," Walt later said. "People were not afraid to veer from the path and leave their own

Walt "Clyde" Frazier

footprints. Everybody was looking to create this niche, to be different in some way."

Walt came to the Knicks in 1967 from Southern Illinois University. He joined the great center, and Knicks captain, Willis Reed, to bring New York back to respectability after years of losing.

In 1970, Walt and Willis combined with Hall of Famers Bill Bradley and Dave DeBusschere, plus Phil Jackson and Cazzie Russell, to finally bring New York an NBA title. Then in 1972, the Knicks acquired one of the league's flashiest players, Earl "The Pearl" Monroe. Clyde and "The Pearl" became the coolest backcourt in NBA history. They thrilled the sold-out crowds in Madison Square Garden.

George Gervin

The dazzling styles of today's stars like Allen Iverson, Jason Kidd and Stephon Marbury started with Clyde and The Pearl. "One of the things I learned early in my career, even in college, was how to play to the crowd," Monroe said. "It became important to have the crowd on my side. It just made my juices flow. The things I did on the court a lot of times were instinctive. But at the same time, I knew exactly what we were doing as a team."

But Julius Erving was the man everyone was whispering about—the legendary Dr. J. He was style, he was grace, he could fly. Unfortunately for the NBA, Dr. J played in the rival American Basketball Association. But in 1976, Doc joined the Philadelphia 76ers, and the NBA would never be the same again.

NBA stars had played above the rim before, but no one could do it like Dr. J. "It was psychological," he once said. "If we were down a few points and I'm fast-breaking toward the hoop, I'd sometimes decide the time had come to get freaky. It got the crowd up. It got the team up. It got me up." Dr. J was more than just a great player. He was a favorite with fans no matter where he played. A game against Doc and the 76ers always guaranteed a large crowd. Dr. J was second only to Muhammad Ali as the most popular African-American athlete in America.

The 1970s also featured other exciting African-American players like Elvin Hayes and Wes Unseld of the Washington Bullets; Nate "Tiny" Archibald and Jo Jo White of the Boston Celtics; Bob Lanier of the Detroit Pistons; Artis Gilmore of the Chicago Bulls; George "The Iceman" Gervin of the San Antonio Spurs; Maurice Lucas of the Portland Trail Blazers; Marques Johnson of the

Milwaukee Bucks; George McGinnis of the Philadelphia 76ers; and Bob McAdoo of the Buffalo Braves.

African-Americans were also taking important steps off the court. In 1971, Wayne Embry was named general manager of the Milwaukee Bucks—the first African-American to take that position. Almost 25 years later, in 1994, Wayne also became the first African-American team president when he took over the Cleveland Cavaliers.

In 1975, Al Attles became the second African-American head coach to win an NBA title when he guided the Golden State Warriors past the Washington Bullets. And in 1979, Lenny Wilkens ended the decade by coaching the Seattle SuperSonics to an NBA title.

But the NBA also faced some of its most serious problems during the '70s. Although the games were exciting, attendance had fallen dramatically. Television broadcasted the NBA Finals on delayed videotape after the local news. It was not even on live TV.

Many people wondered whether fans would buy tickets to watch a sports league with an increasing number of African-American players. "It's race, pure and simple," one team official once said. "No major sport comes up against it the way we do. It's just difficult to get a lot of people to watch huge, intelligent, millionaire black people on television."

There were even suggestions that the league had too many black players and could not appeal to a white audience. That put added pressure on the African-American players. "It was being made out to be a negative," former African-American NBA star Marques Johnson said. "People were saying that the league was failing because of black players.

Dennis Johnson

"It got to the point for me that I once bought a Halloween mask of a white person and was going to wear it during an exhibition game. I was frustrated, so I wanted to make the point that if you wanted more white faces, here is another white face. It was a white face on a black guy, but it was still a white face. My teammates talked me out of it. My question about what was being said was, why? I thought the NBA wanted the best players, whether they were black or white." Racism wasn't as prevalent as it was in the 1950s and 1960s, but there was still an undercurrent of racism throughout the league, and a lot of African-American players had a hard time dealing with that.

Another problem the league faced was drug abuse. In the 1970s, drug abuse became a big problem and, unfortunately, some players in the NBA started using drugs. Because the league was predominantly African-American, this not only made the players look bad but it also made all African-Americans look bad.

By the end of the '70s, the NBA was struggling to survive. It was reported that 17 of the 23 teams were losing money. No one was watching the games on television. The league needed help.

It got Magic and Larry Legend.

KEY MOMENTS OF THE 1970s

March 30, 1971—A Los Angeles County judge rules that the NBA cannot prevent Seattle SuperSonics rookie Spencer Haywood from playing. Haywood's lawsuit ended the NBA's rule against allowing collegiate underclassmen to join the league.

1971—Wayne Embry is named general manager of the Milwaukee Bucks, becoming the first African-American to hold that position in the NBA.

1974—Ray Scott of the Detroit Pistons is named Coach of the Year. He was the first African-American to be named Coach of the Year in any sport.

1974—Bill Russell becomes the first African-American NBA player inducted into the Naismith Memorial Basketball Hall of Fame.

1974—Wilt Chamberlain retires from the Los Angeles Lakers with more than 31,000 career points and 23,000 career rebounds.

May 25, 1975—The Golden State Warriors beat the Washington Bullets 96–95 in Game 4 of the NBA Finals, making Al Attles the second African-American coach to win an NBA championship.

June 17, 1976—The Denver Nuggets, Indiana Pacers, New York Nets and San Antonio Spurs are absorbed into the NBA, eliminating the rival American Basketball Association.

October 20, 1976—The New York Nets sell superstar Julius Erving's contract to the Philadelphia 76ers.

June 1979—Michigan State sophomore guard Earvin "Magic" Johnson is selected first overall by the Los Angeles Lakers in the NBA Draft.

CHAPTER 6

Magic and Larry Save the Day

Earvin Johnson and Larry Bird were as different as two basketball players could possibly be. Earvin was a 6-9 African-American point guard from Lansing, Michigan. His ballhandling skills and incredible passing ability earned him the nickname "Magic" while he was at Michigan State University.

Larry was a 6-9 white forward from French Lick, Indiana. His great shooting, passing and all-around skills made him a star at Indiana State University.

These two players first became famous in 1979 when Magic's Michigan State Spartans defeated Larry's Indiana State Sycamores in the NCAA Championship game. Because of the exciting rivalry between Magic and Larry, more people watched that game on television than any other NCAA Championship game. So when Magic announced that he was leaving Michigan State early and would enter the NBA at that same time as Larry, people began to get excited about the NBA again.

Larry became a member of the Boston Celtics, while

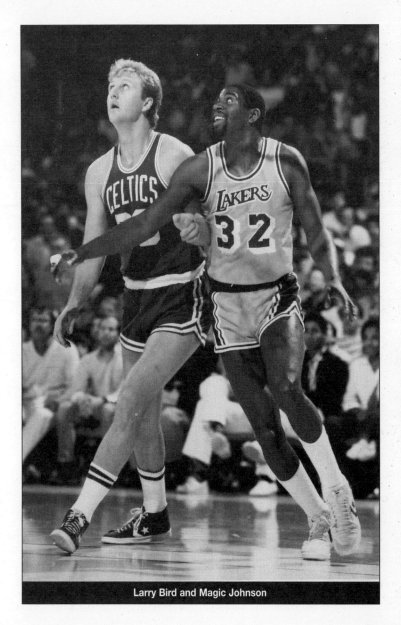

Larry Bird and Magic Johnson

Magic Johnson

Magic joined the Los Angeles Lakers. The competition between those two teams quickly became the greatest rivalry in NBA history. Not only was it Lakers against the Celtics, it was an African-American star competing against a white star. It was a West Coast city against an East Coast city. Magic vs. Larry had everything the NBA needed to get fans interested again.

"When a game was coming up, people were prepared in both cities," Magic Johnson said of the Lakers/Celtics rivalry. "When we hit [Boston], it was like the devil had come to town. You'd hear guys at the airport say 'Magic, Larry is going to kill you. There's no Magic here.' It was so intense. And when the Celtics came to L.A., the same thing happened to them."

In his rookie season, Magic teamed with the great Kareem Abdul-Jabbar to lead the Lakers to their first NBA title since Wilt Chamberlain and Jerry West had won in 1972. Magic was named MVP of the NBA Finals, but Larry was named NBA Rookie of the Year.

In 1981, the Celtics made it to the Finals, but the Lakers did not. Larry won his first title when Boston defeated the Houston Rockets and their great African-American center Moses Malone.

The next year, it was the Lakers who made the Finals, but the Celtics were missing. Magic, along with Kareem, beat Julius Erving and the Philadelphia 76ers in the Finals.

Magic and Larry had been in the league three seasons, but they had yet to meet in the Finals. The anticipation of that matchup drew more fans to the NBA. Because of the popularity of Magic and Larry, the NBA became a big

Bernard King

show for television again.

The popularity of Magic and Larry allowed other African-Americans to become noticed as stars. Moses Malone had entered into the rival ABA right out Petersburg (Virginia) High, but became one the NBA's 50 greatest players while starring with the Houston Rockets and Philadelphia 76ers. In 1983, Moses helped Dr. J and the Sixers finally win an NBA title.

Celtics center Robert Parish was called "The Chief." He starred with Larry Bird and Kevin McHale on three championship teams. He ended his 20-year career by winning a title with Michael Jordan and the Chicago Bulls in 1997.

Other stars who debuted during the Magic and Larry era include the high-scoring Alex English of the Denver Nuggets; Maurice Cheeks of the 76ers; point guard Dennis Johnson, who won one title with the Seattle SuperSonics and two with the Boston Celtics; guard Norm Nixon, who won two titles with Magic and the Lakers; classy Sidney Moncrief of the Milwaukee Bucks; Bernard King of the New York Knicks and Adrian Dantley of the Utah Jazz.

"These were the players who brought the game to life for my generation," Phoenix Suns All-Star guard and 2000 USA Olympian Jason Kidd said. "These were the stars that we watched on television.

"But there were guys before them who didn't have the opportunity to be seen as much on TV, but they set the foundation for Dr. J and Magic and Michael Jordan. Then those guys opened the doors for us."

Another important NBA addition came in 1984, when David Stern replaced Larry O'Brien as the league's commissioner. With Stern in charge, the NBA began an aggressive campaign to promote its star players, whether they were white or African-American.

"People said that America would not accept a sport played predominantly by black men," Stern said. "We never believed that. You've got to understand the impact our players had on this country. People loved them."

Basketball fans finally got what they wanted to see in the 1984 NBA Finals: Magic's Lakers and Larry's Celtics met. The series went seven games, with the Celtics winning 111–102 in Boston.

The next season, the Celtics and Lakers met again in the Finals. This time it was Magic who celebrated the championship as the Lakers won in six games. Magic and Larry had the last of their three NBA championship encounters in 1987. Once again, Magic and the Lakers won in six games.

When Larry and Magic first entered the league, some games in the NBA Finals were shown on television on tape-delay. Their last Finals encounter in 1987 was televised live to 27 different countries. For the record, Magic led the Lakers to five NBA titles while Larry led the Celtics to three.

It is true that part of the interest in the rivalry between these two players was because one was black and the other was white. But together, these two great players saved the NBA. And in a strange way, their large appeal to fans everywhere helped to make the NBA color-blind.

"It's hard to look at a white man and see black," Magic once said, "But when I look at Larry, that's what I see. I see myself."

Bob Lanier

CHAPTER 7

Air of Greatness

Thanks to Magic Johnson and Larry Bird, the NBA had become more popular than ever before. There were established African-American star players, and more were coming into the league each year. But in 1984, the star of all stars started to shine over the NBA.

Michael Jordan wasn't the first player selected in the 1984 NBA Draft. Hakeem Olajuwon, a Nigerian center from the University of Houston, was considered the top player and was picked first by the Houston Rockets.

A year earlier the Portland Trail Blazers had drafted guard Clyde Drexler, so in 1984 they drafted center Sam Bowie from the University of Kentucky with the second pick.

With the third pick, the Chicago Bulls knew they could not pass up Michael Jordan, the University of North Carolina guard who had been the most exciting player in college basketball.

"After Chicago drafted him, I coached a team of NBA guys against the 1984 Olympic team with Jordan," former Philadelphia 76ers coach Billy Cunningham said. "In that game, Jordan was phenomenal, a man playing with boys. I had guys coming to the timeout huddle saying, 'You've got to be kidding.' Michael was that good."

Michael Jordan

Michael Jordan

In his first season, Michael averaged 28.2 points, 6.5 rebounds and 5.9 assists to become the NBA Rookie of the Year. During his third season, Michael averaged 37.1 points and won his first of seven straight scoring titles.

But as big as Michael was on the court, he was even bigger off the court. Julius Erving had proven that an African-American could be the most popular player with fans, but Michael took it to another level.

Nike took a chance that Jordan was going to be great, and signed him to a shoe contract as soon as he announced he was leaving North Carolina. His signature shoe was called the Air Jordan, and it became the most popular basketball shoe of all time.

Michael wasn't just popular. He was popular with everyone. People of every race, men and women, parents and children, young people and old, all loved Michael. His advertising campaign with Gatorade had everyone singing, "If I could be like Mike."

"All of us wanted to take off from the free-throw line and dunk after we saw Michael do it," Minnesota superstar forward Kevin Garnett said. "I think he inspired every young kid in America. The first time we played the Bulls was something I'll never forget. I kept thinking, 'I'm playing against Michael Jordan.' It was a thrill."

By the time Michael finished his career, he had led the Bulls to six NBA titles, become one of the most famous athletes on the planet and been named the Greatest Athlete of the 20th Century.

Michael was the best, but the 1980s also introduced some of the most famous African-American basketball players of all time. Of the 31 African-Americans selected as one of the 50 Greatest Players in NBA History, nine entered the league in the 1980s.

Isiah Lord Thomas led Indiana University to the NCAA title as a sophomore in 1981, then entered the NBA. As the heart and soul of the Detroit Pistons, Thomas won back-to-back NBA titles between Magic Johnson's last and Michael Jordan's first.

Although he was just 6-1, 185 pounds, Isiah's fierce competitive nature made him one of the greatest performers in the sport. "Once it's time to take care of business, all that other stuff you put on the side," Isiah once said about playing in the NBA. "You and I might be friends off the court, but on the court you better do what you need to get done out there or we're going to be adversaries."

Two years before Jordan came into the league, the Los Angeles Lakers drafted Jordan's North Carolina teammate James Worthy first overall in 1982. "Big Game" James helped the Lakers win three NBA titles. In Game 7 of the 1988 NBA Finals, he had a triple-double—36 points, 16 rebounds and 10 assists—against the Detroit Pistons, and was named Finals MVP.

The Portland Trail Blazers were criticized for not selecting Jordan, but Clyde "The Glide" Drexler was also one of the NBA's most exciting guards. He eventually joined his

Isiah Thomas

Charles Barkley

Scottie Pippen

Karl Malone

former college teammate Hakeem Olajuwon in Houston and won an NBA title with the Rockets.

In Philadelphia, the 76ers drafted an overweight forward from Auburn University named Charles Barkley. After losing weight, he got rid of his nickname "The Round Mound of Rebound" and, despite being just 6-6 (although many didn't think he was taller than 6-4½), became one the best forwards to ever play.

"My body was not meant to play the way I do,"Charles Barkley said. "I'm shorter than most of the guys who play up front in the NBA, the guys who play elbow wars every night. I've always known that someday it would take its toll, that my body would just give in to the pounding. But that was okay. It was a sacrifice I had decided to make. The bumps, bruises, strains and sprains would heal up when I was through."

Karl Malone earned his nickname "The Mailman" because he always delivered while playing at Louisiana Tech University. In 1985, the Utah Jazz drafted Malone, a player who might be the best power forward of all time.

Scottie Pippen, who had played college ball at little-known Central Arkansas, was selected by the Seattle SuperSonics but immediately traded to the Chicago Bulls. In Scottie, Michael Jordan found a running mate. Scottie was by Michael's side for all of the Bulls' six championships.

"Scottie Pippen has got to be considered one of the best all-around players in the game," Jordan once said of his longtime teammate. "When one phase of his game is not on key, he's able to contribute in other ways. That's a sign of greatness."

They called David Robinson "The Admiral" while he

was winning NCAA Player of the Year honors at the U.S. Naval Academy. David was the first overall pick in the 1987 NBA Draft, but he served two years in the Navy before joining the San Antonio Spurs. With the help of young superstar Tim Duncan, David led the Spurs to the NBA title the year after Jordan retired.

Other stars of the 1980s included Mark Aguirre of the Dallas Mavericks and Detroit Pistons; Dominique Wilkins, of the Atlanta Hawks; Rolando Blackman of the Dallas Mavericks; and silky-sweet shooting Alex English of the Denver Nuggets.

"I remember watching all these guys when I was growing up," said Los Angeles Lakers star Kobe Bryant, who was just 18 when he came into the NBA. "And then suddenly, I'm playing against them in the NBA. It was an amazing feeling."

By the end of the 1980s, close to 80 percent of the players in the NBA were African-American. The league was also leading the way in the hiring of African-American coaches and front-office officials.

When the decade had started, the NBA was on the verge of collapsing. When it ended, the NBA had grown from 22 to 27 teams and trailed only the National Football League in popularity. "I'm very proud of the fact that we never believed the notion that America would not support great athletes because of the color of their skin," NBA commissioner David Stern said. "What I think says the most about how far America has come is that it's not even an issue anymore when a minority is hired in the NBA."

With great African-American stars in the forefront, the NBA had captured the heart of America. Now it was ready to go after the world.

KEY MOMENTS OF THE 1980s

June 19, 1984—The Chicago Bulls and the Philadelphia 76ers select Michael Jordan and Charles Barkley respectively in the first round of the NBA Draft.

June 1985—Georgetown center Patrick Ewing is selected number one overall by the New York Knicks in the first NBA Draft Lottery.

June 8, 1986—The Boston Celtics defeat the Houston Rockets 114–97 in Game 6 as K.C. Jones joins former teammate Bill Russell as the only African-American coaches to win two NBA titles.

June 13, 1989—The Los Angeles Lakers lose Game 4 of the NBA Finals to the Detroit Pistons, marking the end of Kareem Abdul-Jabbar's career.

November 1989—Center David Robinson, who had been drafted number one overall in 1987 by the San Antonio Spurs, joins the NBA after serving a two-year military commitment.

CHAPTER 8

The American Dream

It was the summer of 1992, and the Olympic Games would be held in Barcelona, Spain. For the first time ever, the International Olympic Committee had voted to allow professional basketball players to compete in the Olympic Games. The players who had been selected to represent the United States were called the "Dream Team."

Although many Americans thought the United States was sending professional players to the Olympics because the 1988 team had lost the gold medal to the former Soviet Union, it was actually the rest of the world who wanted NBA players to play. The international game had advanced considerably, and the best players, who were in their late 20s or early 30s, were better than U.S. players who were in their late teens or early 20s.

But the victories the international teams were achieving were not as meaningful to them because they knew that they were not playing the best players in the world. So other countries voted to remove all restrictions and allow every player in the world to be eligible for the Olympics.

USA Basketball put together its first Olympic team in 1992, and it was such a great collection of players that it

The Dream Team

The Dream Team

was commonly called the Dream Team. Eight of the 12 players on the team were African-Americans—Michael Jordan, Magic Johnson, Charles Barkley, Clyde Drexler, David Robinson, Karl Malone, Patrick Ewing and Scottie Pippen. The remainder of the team was made up of Larry Bird, Chris Mullin, John Stockton and Christian Laettner.

"I wanted that gold medal more than anything," Magic Johnson said after the Olympics. "The library would be complete. It was closed because I won everything from Pop Warner on up. The Olympics might even be bigger than winning the NBA title because it was worldwide."

Before the Dream Team, basketball was played in many parts of the world, but there was a great fascination with American basketball. Every so often, a great international player would come to a United States college and develop into a player good enough to play in the NBA.

"I started playing basketball when I was seventeen," said Nigerian-born center Hakeem Olajuwon of the Houston Rockets who, in 1984, became the first non-United States citizen to be picked first overall in the NBA Draft. "I had played soccer in Nigeria since I was two or three years old, but all my friends told me I was too tall to play soccer. I didn't know anything about basketball until I met the coach of the Nigerian National Team. I couldn't dunk for a couple of weeks, but I started getting interested in basketball."

Because of the fascination with American basketball, the Dream Teamers were the stars of the Barcelona Olympics. With a few exceptions, like the great track star Jesse Owens and boxer Muhammad Ali, few African-American athletes have made a bigger impression on the rest of the world than the members of the Dream Team.

"It seemed that most of the other teams did not think of themselves as opponents," NBA deputy commissioner Russ Granik once said of the Dream Team. "I remember one guy was guarding Magic Johnson during a game, and he kept asking if he could have Magic's jersey after the game. For them, it was a dream come true just to be on the same court with the greatest players in the world."

The Dream Team's performance in the Olympics helped the popularity of the NBA worldwide, and many of the African-American stars became as popular in other countries as they already were in America.

"When I was growing up, Scottie Pippen was my role model," said Dallas Mavericks forward Dirk Nowitzki, who is from Germany. "He was the player I wanted to be like." The NBA had finally spread across the world.

The Changing of the Guard

Throughout the 1980s and most of the 1990s, the NBA was dominated by African-American stars like Michael Jordan, Charles Barkley, Karl Malone, David Robinson and Patrick Ewing.

But other stars, like Seattle SuperSonics guard Gary Payton, Indiana Pacers sweet-shooting guard Reggie Miller, Cleveland Cavaliers mad-dunking forward Shawn Kemp and former Chicago Bulls forward Dennis Rodman also made names for themselves. By the '80s, no one would ever again say the NBA was "too black" for American society.

But change is the only constant in sports. As the older stars began to leave the league, a new generation of African-American stars had to step into their places. Los Angeles Lakers center Shaquille O'Neal was named to the NBA 50th Anniversary All-Time Team after playing less than four full seasons in the league. The 7-1, 320-pound star is being compared with Wilt Chamberlain, Bill Russell and Kareem Abdul-Jabbar as one of the greatest centers of all time. In the 1999–2000 season, he guided the Lakers to the NBA title and joined Jordan and Willis Reed as the only player to be named All-Star MVP, league

MVP and NBA Finals MVP all in the same season.

With Shaq, Miami Heat center Alonzo Mourning, San Antonio Spurs center/forward Tim Duncan, Sacramento Kings forward Chris Webber, Portland Trail Blazers forward Rasheed Wallace and Denver Nuggets forward Antonio McDyess, the NBA has continued its great tradition of dominating big men.

Then there are Kevin Garnett of the Minnesota

Shaquille O'Neal

Timberwolves and Kobe Bryant of the Los Angeles Lakers, who were told they were not ready to make the jump to the NBA directly from high school. But both made their first NBA All-Star team in their second seasons. Philadelphia 76ers high-scoring guard Allen Iverson is already being called one of the most exciting NBA players ever, while Phoenix Suns guard Jason Kidd, Milwaukee Bucks guard Ray Allen, New Jersey Nets guard Stephon Marbury and Houston Rockets rookie Steve Francis continue the legacy of great guards like Isiah Thomas and Nate Archibald.

Magic Johnson created a new position for players big enough to be forwards but skilled enough to play like guards. Grant Hill, Anfernee "Penny" Hardaway, Shareef Abdur-Rahim, Vince Carter, Tracy McGrady, Eddie Jones, Michael Finley and Jalen Rose are some of the most versatile players to ever be in the league.

Today, basketball fans on every continent know the names of the top players in the NBA. Fifty years after it finally let African-American players into the league, the NBA now features some of the most popular, well-paid and respected African-American athletes in the world.

"The league has come a long way," said Indiana point guard Travis Best. "I think a lot of it is the fact that people know and love the game of basketball. That's what it's really all about. I think all people appreciate the athletes and what they do on the court every night." Although they don't face the hardships of the early African-American pioneers in the game, today's NBA players are not totally immune from being young African-American men in the United States.

"A reality that kids today have to understand is that there are certain elements in our society that are not as scrutinized as others," said former NBA star Marques Johnson. "Athletes, actors and musicians kind of fall into a category where they seem to be embraced regardless of color. But what happens is, when they make a mistake or do something that is considered out of the norm, it becomes open house on them—a field day."

Many of the young African-American stars in the NBA are finding out there are many expectations and a lot of pressure that comes along with being a high-profile athlete. "I'm human," said the 76ers young star Allen Iverson who, at times, has been criticized for everything from his hairstyle to his clothes to his friends. "People want to think that I'm perfect or can't make mistakes, but I'm not. I'm human. I make mistakes just like everyone else."

When Kevin Garnett entered the NBA Draft in 1995 right out of Chicago's Farragut Academy, he became the first player in 20 years to go directly to the NBA from high school. Garnett's success with the Minnesota Timberwolves led to many other players entering the NBA without spending time in college. Now the question about NBA players is whether they are old enough and

Kevin Garnett

mature enough to handle the responsibilities that go along with fulfilling their dreams. Everyone understands that the players are younger, but when owners are paying them millions of dollars and fans are paying a lot of money for tickets, there is a lot of pressure to grow up fast.

Many people say that the NBA is a man's game, and if young players don't want to deal with adult responsibilities, they should wait before joining the league. "The whole league has to grow up," former NBA star Magic Johnson said. "Doing whatever it takes to get the job done goes with the privilege and responsibility of being a star." Those responsibilities extend beyond the court.

Today's NBA players—particularly the young African-Americans—are asked to do a lot more than play basketball. Basketball players have a big presence in the African-American community. And whether they like it or not, they are considered role models and expected to act in a certain way. Former NBA star Charles Barkley once tried to explain that "he was not a role model," but no one listened to him.

"It is a challenge," Phoenix Suns star guard Jason Kidd said of the responsibilities of being a famous athlete. "As a kid when you're growing up, all you're thinking about is playing basketball. But it is a lot more than that once you get here. Today, you see athletes spotlighted more than ever on and off the basketball court. As a kid, there is nothing that can prepare you for everything that you are going to go through in the NBA life. As a kid, all you wanted to do was play basketball. Now there are responsibilities that come with that."

There is a price for being highly paid and famous. People expect NBA players to give back to the community and to use their influence and wealth to make things better for other people.

But sometimes it seems that no matter how much a player does, it is never enough. "There are pros and cons of everything," Detroit Pistons guard/forward Jerry Stackhouse said. "I've worked hard to become an NBA player, but if you look at it I really only work two or three hours each day of the week. The everyday person is working nine to five every day, and they don't receive the many benefits I have. Yes, we are scrutinized more, but I think it's fair. That's part of the price you have to pay for being a celebrity."

Often, criticism comes because people don't truly

know the type of things NBA players do to give back to their communities. "Whenever I do stuff in the community, it's because I want to do it, not because I want attention," Lakers center Shaquille O'Neal said. "I'm the type of person who will never let a bunch of suits come in the office and say, 'Okay, you need to go to this hospital, you need to sign autographs, you need to do this or that.'

Allen Iverson

"Whenever I do something, it's from the heart. I do it because that's how I was taught to be by my parents. I don't do things for media purposes or to try to get people to like me."

Most NBA players do feel a tremendous sense of responsibility to give back to their communities. The list of charities they contribute to and good deeds that they do would be too long to write.

"I've been so richly blessed, and only a small percentage of children have had the opportunities that I've had," said Toronto Raptors star Vince Carter. "Now that I am in a position to do things, I feel I have to give back."

Golden State Warriors forward Antawn Jamison, who is very active in the communities of Oakland and San Francisco, agrees. "As basketball players, we have almost everything we can dream of having," he said. "But you have other people who are really struggling. It might make a difference in their lives if you just go out and visit with them. A lot of people look up to us because we are NBA players. We have to realize that and because of that, it's almost like our duty to try and make a difference.

Antawn Jamison

"I always told myself that no matter how successful I became as a basketball player or in life in general, I would always go back into the community and spend time with people who may benefit from my being there."

Still, for many of today's young players, fame and fortune has not kept them from also being viewed as young African-American men, and being judged for that. America has changed greatly since African-Americans had to use separate bathrooms and water fountains, but there is still a long way to go before the color barrier is completely broken.

"This generation is just bringing a different type of flow to the NBA," said Los Angeles Lakers star Kobe Bryant. "A lot of people around the league are not used to it, particularly off the court. Our style of dress is different. The way we relate to each other is different. Some people react badly to this...But you just need to understand that we are just a bunch of young guys who love to play basketball and have fun.

"Still, you have to remind yourself that kids do look up to you whether you want them to or not. You have to accept that and handle yourself in a professional manner. I'm just living my dream. If people want to make me out as a role model and add that to my responsibilities, that's fine."

Not that long ago, the NBA didn't allow African-American players into the league because they were afraid that people wouldn't pay money to watch them play. But in 1950, three brave African-American men—Chuck Cooper, Earl Lloyd and Nat "Sweetwater" Clifton— accepted the challenge to become the first. Over the next 50 years, many great African-American basketball stars fought hard and made sacrifices to change society's view of African-Americans and to open the door for future African-American stars.

As we enter the 21st century, the NBA is now predominantly made up of African-American players, and it is one of the most popular professional sports leagues on the planet. NBA stars are admired worldwide because they are marvelous basketball players, regardless of the color of their skin.

"I think we sometimes forget how far we've come," said Jason Kidd. "A lot of people worked hard so that today's players could make our dreams come true. It's now up to us to make sure this thing keeps growing so the next generation will be able to make theirs come true."

KEY MOMENTS OF THE 1990s

June 12, 1991—The Chicago Bulls defeat the Los Angeles Lakers, 108–101, in Game 5 of the NBA Finals to win the first of six championships. Michael Jordan averages 31.2 points, 11.4 assists and 6.6 rebounds and is named Finals MVP.

November 7, 1991—Los Angeles Lakers star Earvin "Magic" Johnson retires after announcing that he has tested positive for HIV, the virus that causes AIDS.

August 1, 1992—The Dream Team defeats Croatia 117–85 to win the Gold Medal at the Barcelona (Spain) Olympics.

October 6, 1993—Michael Jordan retires from the NBA after winning three straight championships with the Chicago Bulls.

1994—Wayne Embry is named President/Chief Operating Officer of the Cleveland Cavaliers, becoming the first African-American to be made team president in NBA history.

March 18, 1995—Michael Jordan ends his retirement and returns to the NBA.

June 1995—Then-19-year-old Kevin Garnett is drafted fifth overall out of Chicago's Farragut Academy, making him the first player in 20 years to enter the NBA directly out of high school.

January 13, 1999—Michael Jordan retires from the NBA after winning six championships with the Chicago Bulls.

GREAT AFRICAN-AMERICAN PLAYERS OF THE 20TH CENTURY

GREAT PLAYERS OF THE 1950s

Don Barksdale (1951–1955): Height: 6-6, Weight: 200, College: Marin JC/UCLA. First African-American to play in an All-Star Game (1953). Played two seasons with Baltimore Bullets and two seasons with Boston Celtics. Played in 262 games, averaging 11 points and 8 rebounds.

Nat "Sweetwater" Clifton (1950–1958): Height: 6-7½, Weight: 235, College: Xavier. Played seven seasons with New York Knicks and one season with Detroit Pistons. Appeared in 544 games, averaging 10 points and 8.2 rebounds. Made one All-Star team.

Chuck Cooper (1950–1956): Height: 6-5, Weight: 215, College: West Virginia State/Duquesne. First African-American to be drafted by an NBA team. Played four seasons with Boston Celtics, one season with Milwaukee Hawks, split final season with St. Louis Hawks and Ft. Wayne Pistons. Appeared in 409 games, averaging 6.7 points and 5.9 rebounds.

Earl "Big Cat" Lloyd (1950–1960): Height: 6-6, Weight: 220, College: West Virginia State. First African-American to appear in an NBA game. Played one season with Washington Capitols, six seasons with Syracuse Nationals and two seasons with Detroit Pistons. Appeared in 560 games, averaging 8.4 points and 6.4 rebounds.

GREAT PLAYERS OF THE 1960s

Elgin Baylor (1958–1972): Height: 6-5, Weight: 225, College: College of Idaho/Seattle University. First African-American player to be drafted No. 1 overall. Played 14 seasons with Minneapolis/Los Angeles Lakers. Appeared in 846 games, averaging 27.4 points and 13.5 rebounds. Played in 11 All-Star games. Holds NBA Finals Record for most points in one game (61 against the Boston Celtics in 1962). Member of NBA 50th Anniversary All-Time Team.

Walt Bellamy (1961–1973): Height: 6-10½, Weight: 245, College: Indiana. Drafted first overall by Chicago Packers. Played 14 seasons with Chicago Zephyrs, Baltimore Bullets, New York Knicks, Detroit Pistons, Atlanta Hawks and New Orleans Jazz. Appeared in 1,043 games, averaging 20.1 points and 13.7 rebounds.

Wilt Chamberlain (1959–1973): Height: 7-1, Weight: 275, College: Kansas. Played six seasons with Philadelphia/San Francisco Warriors, four seasons with Philadelphia 76ers and five seasons with Los Angeles Lakers. Appeared in 1,045 games, averaging 30.1 points and 22.9 rebounds. Played in 13 All-Star games. Scored 100 points in one game, and had 55 rebounds in another. Never fouled out of a game. Member of NBA 50th Anniversary All-Time Team.

Hal Greer (1958–1973): Height: 6-2, Weight: 175, College: Marshall. Played five seasons with Syracuse Nationals, and eight seasons with Philadelphia 76ers. Appeared in 1,122 games, averaging 19.2 points, 5 rebounds and 4 assists. Member of NBA 50th Anniversary All-Time Team.

Sam Jones (1957–1969): Height: 6-4, Weight: 205, College: North Carolina Central. Played 12 seasons with Boston Celtics. Appeared in 871 games, averaging 17.7 points and 4.9 rebounds. Member of 10 NBA Championship teams. Member of NBA 50th Anniversary All-Time Team.

Willis Reed (1964–1973): Height: 6-9½, Weight: 235, College: Grambling State. Played 10 seasons with New York Knicks. Appeared in 650 games, averaging 18.7 points and 12.9 rebounds. Won two NBA titles with Knicks. First player to be named League MVP, All-Star Game MVP and NBA Finals MVP in the same season (1970). Member of NBA 50th Anniversary All-Time Team.

Oscar Robertson (1960–1973): Height: 6-5, Weight: 210, College: Cincinnati. Played 10 seasons with Cincinnati Royals and three seasons with Milwaukee Bucks. Appeared in 1,040 games, averaging 25.7 points, 7.5 rebounds, 9.5 assists. Averaged triple-double in 1961-62 season. 12-time All-Star. Member of NBA 50th Anniversary All-Time Team.

Bill Russell (1956–1969): Height: 6-9½, Weight: 220, College: San Francisco. First African-American to be league MVP (1958). First African-American head coach (1966). First African-American head coach to win NBA Championship (1968). Played 13 seasons with Boston Celtics. Appeared in 963 games, averaging 15.1 points, 22.5 rebounds. Member of 11 NBA Championship teams. 12-time All-Star. Member of NBA 50th Anniversary All-Time Team.

Nate Thurmond (1963–1977): Height: 6-11, Weight: 230, College: Bowling Green. Played 11 seasons with San Francisco/Golden State Warriors, two seasons with Chicago Bulls and two seasons with Cleveland Cavaliers. Appeared in 964 games, averaging 15.0 points and 15.0 rebounds. Member of NBA 50th Anniversary All-Time Team.

Lenny Wilkens (1960–1975): Height: 6-1, Weight: 185, College: Providence. Played eight seasons with St. Louis Hawks, four seasons with Seattle SuperSonics, two seasons with Cleveland Cavaliers and one season with Portland Trail Blazers. Appeared in 1,077 games, averaging 16.5 points and 6.7 assists. Won the most games as a coach in NBA history. Coached 1996 United States Olympic Team to a Gold Medal. One of two people to be in the Basketball Hall of Fame as both a player and coach. Member of NBA 50th Anniversary All-Time Team.

GREAT PLAYERS OF THE 1970s

Kareem Abdul-Jabbar (1969–1989): Height: 7-2, Weight: 230, College: UCLA. Played six seasons with Milwaukee Bucks and 14 seasons with Los Angeles Lakers. Appeared in 1,560 games, averaging 24.6 points and 11.2 rebounds with 3,189 blocked shots. Won three NCAA Championships at UCLA and six NBA Championships. Played in 18 All-Star Games. Member of NBA 50th Anniversary All-Time Team.

Nate "Tiny" Archibald (1970–1984): Height: 6-1, Weight: 160, College: Arizona Western JC/Texas El Paso. Played 13 NBA seasons with the Cincinnati Royals, Kansas City-Omaha Kings, New York Nets, Boston Celtics and Milwaukee Bucks. Appeared in 876 games, averaging 18.8 points and 7.4 assists. Played in six All-Star games. Member of the NBA 50th Anniversary All-Time Team.

Dave Bing (1966–1978): Height: 6-3, Weight: 180, College: Syracuse. Played nine seasons with Detroit Pistons, two seasons with Washington Bullets and one season with Boston Celtics. Appeared in 901 games, averaging 20.3 points and 6.0 assists. Played in seven All-Star games. Member of NBA 50th Anniversary All-Time Team.

Julius "Dr. J" Erving (1971–1976 ABA, 1976–1987 NBA): Height: 6-6½, Weight: 200, College: Massachusetts. Played five seasons in American Basketball Association and 11 seasons with Philadelphia 76ers. Appeared in 407 ABA games averaging 28.7 points and 12.1 rebounds. Appeared in 836 NBA games averaging 22.0 points and 6.7 rebounds. Played in five ABA All-Star games and 11 NBA All-Star games. Member of NBA 50th Anniversary All-Time Team.

Walt "Clyde" Frazier (1967–1980): Height: 6-4, Weight: 200, College: Southern Illinois. Played 10 seasons with New York Knicks and three seasons with Cleveland Cavaliers. Appeared in 825 games averaging 18.9 points, 6.1 assists and 5.9 rebounds. Played in seven All-Star games. Member of NBA 50th Anniversary All-Time Team.

George "Iceman" Gervin (1972–76 ABA, 1976–86 NBA): Height: 6-7. Weight: 185, College: Long Beach State/Eastern Michigan. Played two seasons with Virginia Squires, 12 seasons with San Antonio Spurs and one season with Chicago Bulls. Appeared in 791 NBA games averaging 26.2 points while shooting 51.1 percent. Played in nine NBA All-Star games. Member of NBA 50th Anniversary All-Time Team.

Elvin Hayes (1968–1984): Height: 6-9, Weight: 235, College: Houston. Played seven seasons with the San Diego/Houston Rockets and nine seasons with Baltimore/Capital/Washington Bullets. Appeared in 1,303 games, averaging 21.0 points and 12.5 rebounds. Played in 12 All-Star games. Member of NBA 50th Anniversary All-Time Team.

Bob McAdoo (1972–1986): Height: 6-9, Weight: 210, College: Vincennes (Ind.) J.C./North Carolina. Played 14 seasons with Buffalo Braves, New York Knicks, Boston Celtics, Detroit Pistons, New Jersey Nets, Los Angeles Lakers and Philadelphia 76ers. Appeared in 852 games, averaging 22.1 points and 9.4 rebounds. Shot 50.3 percent.

Earl "The Pearl" Monroe (1967–1980): Height: 6-3½, Weight: 185, College: Winston-Salem State. Played five seasons with Baltimore Bullets and nine season with New York Knicks. Appeared in 926 games, averaging 18.8 points and 3.9 assists. Member of NBA 50th Anniversary All-Time Team.

Wes Unseld (1968–1981): Height: 6-7½, Weight: 245, College: Louisville. Played 13 seasons with Baltimore/Capital/Washington Bullets. Appeared in 984 games, averaging 10.8 points and 14.0 rebounds. Named MVP and Rookie of the Year in 1969. Coached Washington Bullets for seven seasons. Member of NBA 50th Anniversary All-Time Team.

GREAT PLAYERS OF THE 1980s

Charles Barkley (1984–2000): Height: 6-6, Weight: 252, College: Auburn. Played eight seasons with Philadelphia 76ers, four seasons with Phoenix Suns and four seasons with Houston Rockets. Appeared in 1,073 games, averaging 22.1 points and 11.7 rebounds. Played in nine NBA All-Star games. Member of 1992 and 1996 gold medal-winning Olympic Teams. Member of NBA 50th Anniversary All-Time Team.

Adrian Dantley (1976–1991): Height: 6-5, Weight: 210, College: Notre Dame. Played 15 seasons with Buffalo Braves, Indiana Pacers, Los Angeles Lakers, Utah Jazz, Detroit Pistons, Dallas Mavericks and Milwaukee Bucks. Appeared in 955 games, averaging 24.3 points and 5.7 rebounds. Shot 54.5 percent. Played in six All-Star games.

Clyde "The Glide" Drexler (1983–1998): Height: 6-7, Weight: 222, College: Houston. Played 12 seasons with Portland Trail Blazers and four seasons with Houston Rockets. Appeared in 1,086 games, averaging 20.4 points, 6.1 rebounds and 5.6 assists. Member of the 1992 gold medal-winning Olympic Dream Team. Played in nine All-Star games. Member of NBA 50th Anniversary All-Time Team.

Patrick Ewing (1985–still active): Height: 7-0, Weight: 255, College: Georgetown. Has played 15 seasons with New York Knicks. Has appeared in 1,074 games averaging 22.8 points, 10.4 rebounds and 2.65 blocks. Played in nine All-Star games. Member of 1992 gold medal-winning Olympic Dream Team. Member of NBA 50th Anniversary All-Time Team.

Earvin "Magic" Johnson (1979–1991; 1995–1996): Height: 6-9. Weight: 225, College: Michigan State. Played 13 seasons with Los Angeles Lakers. Appeared in 906 games, averaging 19.5 points, 7.2 rebounds and 11.2 assists. Member of five NBA Championship Teams, Member of 1992 gold medal-winning Olympic Dream Team. Played in 11 All-Star games. Member of NBA 50th Anniversary All-Time Team.

Michael Jordan (1984–1993, 1995–1998): Height: 6-6, Weight: 216, College: North Carolina. Played 13 seasons with Chicago Bulls. Appeared in 930 games averaging 31.5 points, 6.3 rebounds and 5.4 assists. Won six NBA titles. Named NBA Finals MVP six times. Named NBA MVP five times. Member of 1992 gold medal-winning Olympic Dream Team. Played in 11 All-Star games. Member of NBA 50th Anniversary All-Time Team.

Karl "The Mailman" Malone (1985–still active): Height: 6-9, Weight: 259, College: Louisiana Tech. Has played 15 seasons with Utah Jazz. Has appeared in 1,192 games averaging 26.0 points and 10.6 rebounds. Twice named NBA MVP. Played in 11 All-Star games. Member of 1992 and 1996 gold medal-winning Olympic Teams. Member of NBA 50th Anniversary All-Time Team.

Moses Malone (1976–1995): Height: 6-10, Weight: 260, College: None. Played 19 seasons with the Buffalo Braves, Houston Rockets, Philadelphia 76ers, Washington Bullets, Atlanta Hawks, Milwaukee Bucks and San Antonio Spurs. Appeared in 1,329 games, averaging 20.6 points and 12.2 rebounds. Played in 11 All-Star games. Member of NBA 50th Anniversary All-Time Team.

Robert Parish (1976–1997): Height: 7-1, Weight: 244, College: Centenary (La.). Played four seasons with Golden State Warriors, 14 seasons with Boston Celtics, two seasons with Charlotte Hornets and one season with Chicago Bulls. Appeared in 1,611 games, averaging 14.5 points and 9.1 rebounds. Played in nine All-Star games. Member of four NBA Championship Teams. Member of NBA 50th Anniversary All-Time Team.

David "The Admiral" Robinson (1989–still active): Height: 7-1, Weight: 250, College: U.S. Naval Academy. Has played 11 seasons with San Antonio Spurs. Appeared in 765 games averaging 23.7 points, 11.3 rebounds and 3.2 blocks. Nine-time All-Star. Member of 1992 and 1996 gold medal-winning Olympic Teams. Member of NBA 50th Anniversary All-Time Team.

Isiah Thomas (1981–1994): Height: 6-1, Weight: 182, College: Indiana. Played 13 seasons with Detroit Pistons. Appeared in 979 games, averaging 19.2 points and 9.3 assists. Played in 11 All-Star games. Member of two NBA Championship Teams. Member of NBA 50th Anniversary All-Time Team.

James Worthy (1982–1994): Height: 6-9, Weight: 225, College: North Carolina. Played 12 seasons with Los Angeles Lakers. Appeared in 926 games, averaging 17.6 points and 5.1 rebounds. Played in seven All-Star games. Member of three NBA Championship Teams. Member of NBA 50th Anniversary All-Time Team.

GREAT PLAYERS OF THE 1990s

Shaquille O'Neal (1992–still active): Height: 7-1, Weight: 320, College: Louisiana State. Has played four seasons with Orlando Magic, four seasons with Los Angeles Lakers. Has appeared in 534 games averaging 27.5 points, 12.4 rebounds and 2.6 blocks. Won 2000 NBA Championship with Los Angeles Lakers. In 2000, joined Willis Reed and Michael Jordan as only players to be named All-Star, League and Finals MVP in same season. Played in six All-Star games. Member of 1996 gold medal-winning Olympic Team. Member of NBA 50th Anniversary All-Time Team.

Gary "The Glove" Payton (1990–still active): Height: 6-4, Weight: 180, College: Oregon State. Has played 10 seasons with Seattle SuperSonics. Has appeared in 786 games averaging 17.2 points, 7.1 assists and 4.1 rebounds. Named to NBA All-Defensive First Team seven times. Played in six All-Star games. Member of 1996 gold medal-winning Olympic Team. Member of 2000 U.S. Olympic Team.

Scottie Pippen (1987–still active): Height: 6-7, Weight: 228, College: Central Arkansas. Has played 11 seasons with Chicago Bulls, one season each with Houston Rockets and Portland Trail Blazers. Has appeared in 965 games averaging 17.3 points, 6.7 rebounds and 5.3 assists. Won six NBA titles with Chicago Bulls. Played in seven All-Star games. Member of 1992 and 1996 gold medal-winning Olympic Teams. Member of NBA 50th Anniversary All-Time Team.